U.S.A. TRAVEL GUIDES

TENNESSEE

BY ANN HEINRICHS • ILLUSTRATED BY MATT KANIA

The Child's World®
childsworld.com

Published by The Child's World®
1980 Lookout Drive • Mankato, MN 56003-1705
800-599-READ • www.childsworld.com

Photo Credits

Photographs ©: iStockphoto, cover, 1, 11; Ken Canning/
iStockphoto, 7; Mark Humphrey/AP Images, 8; Doug
Strickland/Chattanooga Times Free Press/AP Images, 12;
Carol M. Highsmith/Carol M. Highsmith Archive/Library
of Congress, 15, 27; Shiloh National Military Park, 16; J.
Carillet/iStockphoto, 19; Shutterstock Images, 20, 28, 35,
36 (left), 36 (right), Image courtesy of Oak Ridge National
Laboratory, U.S. Dept. of Energy, 23; Darren Brode/
Shutterstock Images, 24; Oliver Gerhard/ImageBROKER
RM/Glow Images, 31; Kenn Stilger/Shutterstock Images,
32

ISBN 9781503819825
LCCN 2016961194

Printing

Printed in the United States of America
PA02334

Ann Heinrichs is the author of more than 100 books for children and young adults. She has also enjoyed successful careers as a children's book editor and an advertising copywriter. Ann grew up in Fort Smith, Arkansas, and lives in Chicago, Illinois.

About the Author
Ann Heinrichs

Matt Kania loves maps and, as a kid, dreamed of making them. In school he studied geography and cartography, and today he makes maps for a living. Matt's favorite thing about drawing maps is learning about the places they represent. Many of the maps he has created can be found in books, magazines, videos, Web sites, and public places.

About the
Map Illustrator
Matt Kania

*On the cover: The Ryman Auditorium in Nashville is
sometimes called the "Mother Church of Country Music."*

OUR TENNESSEE TRIP

TENNESSEE

Let's explore Tennessee! It's a great state for adventure and fun. What will you do in Tennessee? You'll meet **robots**, turtles, and tree frogs. You'll hang out with soldiers in tent camps. You'll see how cars and ice cream are made. You'll hear mountain fiddlers and Cherokee storytellers. You'll float lazily down a river. And you'll explore caves and eat MoonPies!

We'd better get started, so buckle up. It's time to hit the road!

WELCOME TO TENNESSEE

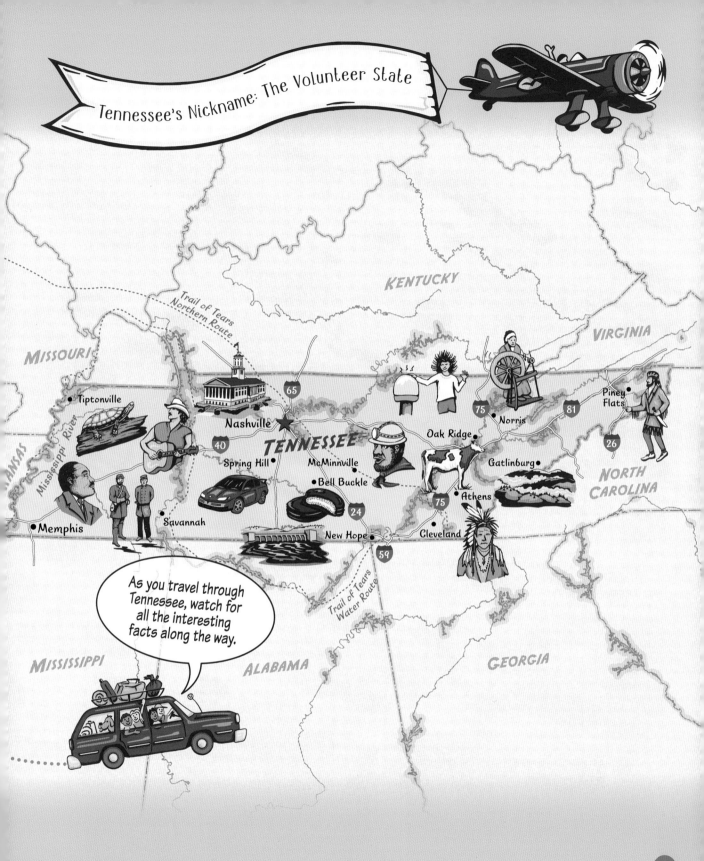

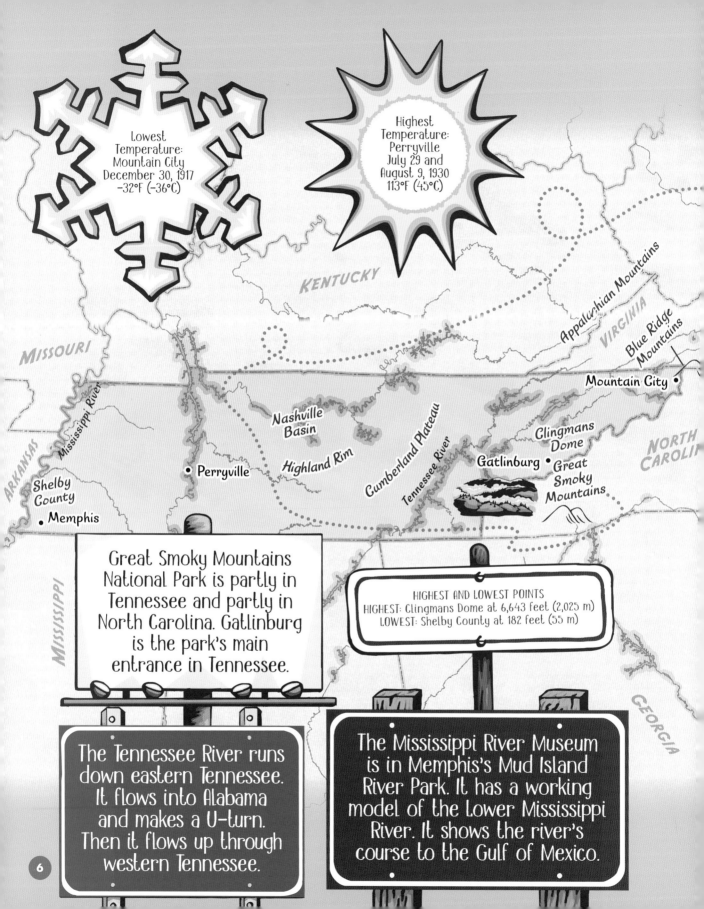

Lowest Temperature:
Mountain City
December 30, 1917
−32°F (−36°C)

Highest Temperature:
Perryville
July 29 and
August 9, 1930
113°F (45°C)

KENTUCKY

MISSOURI

Appalachian Mountains

VIRGINIA

Blue Ridge Mountains

Mountain City

ARKANSAS

Mississippi River

Nashville Basin

Highland Rim

Cumberland Plateau

Tennessee River

Clingmans Dome

Gatlinburg

Great Smoky Mountains

NORTH CAROLINA

Perryville

Shelby County

Memphis

MISSISSIPPI

GEORGIA

Great Smoky Mountains National Park is partly in Tennessee and partly in North Carolina. Gatlinburg is the park's main entrance in Tennessee.

HIGHEST AND LOWEST POINTS
HIGHEST: Clingmans Dome at 6,643 feet (2,025 m)
LOWEST: Shelby County at 182 feet (55 m)

The Tennessee River runs down eastern Tennessee. It flows into Alabama and makes a U-turn. Then it flows up through western Tennessee.

The Mississippi River Museum is in Memphis's Mud Island River Park. It has a working model of the Lower Mississippi River. It shows the river's course to the Gulf of Mexico.

Watch out! We might see black bears in the Smokies. If we do, we should slowly back away.

UP IN THE CLOUDS IN THE SMOKIES

Wander through the Great Smoky Mountains. They're called the Smokies for short. You'll see why they have this name. Low-hanging clouds are all around you. They look like smoke!

The Smokies are part of the Blue Ridge Mountains. These mountains run down Tennessee's eastern edge.

West of here is the valley. The Tennessee River flows through it. Next is the rocky Cumberland Plateau. The Plateau and the Blue Ridge Mountains are part of the Appalachian Mountains.

The Highland Rim is like a big bowl. At the bottom is the Nashville Basin. Then comes another section of the Tennessee River. The Mississippi River forms Tennessee's western border.

Mist rises from the Smokies at sunrise.

SPELUNKING IN CUMBERLAND CAVERNS

Want to go spelunking? That means exploring caves! Check out Cumberland **Caverns**, near McMinnville. It's Tennessee's longest cave system open to the public. Its underground rooms are awesome! One is called the Hall of the Mountain King. It's as big as two football fields!

Wander along the winding passageways. You'll view underground waterfalls and pools. You'll see walls covered with bubbly looking white rocks. Those are calcium deposits sometimes called moon milk. And you'll spot gypsum flowers. These rock formations look like curly vines. When you're done, you'll be an expert spelunker!

Sometimes bands perform in Cumberland Caverns.

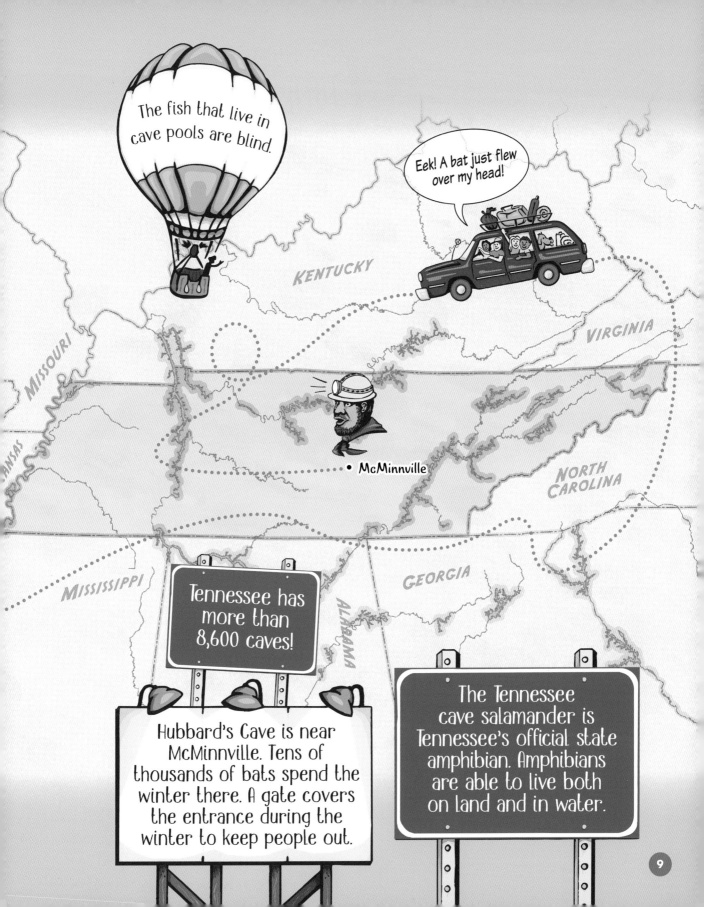

A stinkpot is a musk turtle. It can release a stinky substance to defend itself.

STATE TREE
TULIP POPLAR

STATE BIRD
MOCKINGBIRD

STATE FLOWER
IRIS

Check out all the turtles! No wonder Reelfoot Lake is called the Turtle Capital of the World!

MISSOURI

KENTUCKY

VIRGINIA

Reelfoot Lake

Tiptonville

• Big Sandy

Hustburg •

ARKANSAS

• Perryville

NORTH CAROLINA

Chattanooga •

MISSISSIPPI

GEORGIA

ALABAMA

The National Park Service has 15 sites in Tennessee.

The Tennessee Aquarium is in Chattanooga. It's home to many water creatures, including alligators and sharks.

Reelfoot Lake is Tennessee's largest natural lake. It was created when earthquakes struck in 1811 and 1812.

The Tennessee National Wildlife Refuge has three units. Big Sandy Unit is near Big Sandy. Duck River Unit is near Hustburg. Busseltown Unit is near Perryville.

Want to see some sliders and stinkpots? They're types of turtles! How about river otters? They swim on their backs in the lake. Little green tree frogs are hopping around, too.

You're exploring Reelfoot National Wildlife Refuge! It surrounds Reelfoot Lake. That's in Tennessee's northwest corner, near Tiptonville.

Tennessee has many mountains, forests, rivers, and lakes. And they're full of wildlife! Deer and wild turkeys live there. You'll spot beavers, raccoons, rabbits, and skunks. You'll even see wild hogs in the mountains. Steer clear! They can have a nasty temper!

Keep an eye out for pelicans at Reelfoot Lake.

CHEROKEE HERITAGE FESTIVAL

ap your feet to the steady drumbeat. Watch the fancy dancers leap and swirl. Hear storytellers tell their ancient tales.

You're attending the Cherokee Heritage Festival! It's in Red Clay State Historic Park. That's right on the Georgia border south of Cleveland.

Red Clay was once the Cherokee capital. During the 1800s, the Cherokee adopted many parts of American **culture**. They began using a writing system for their language. They published a Cherokee-language newspaper called the *Cherokee Phoenix.* But the U.S. government wanted Cherokee lands. From 1838 to 1839, the U.S. government forced the Cherokee west to Indian Territory in Oklahoma. The Cherokee did not have enough shelter or food for the journey. Approximately 4,000 Cherokee died. The journey became known as the Trail of Tears.

A man makes a wooden longbow at the Cherokee Heritage Festival.

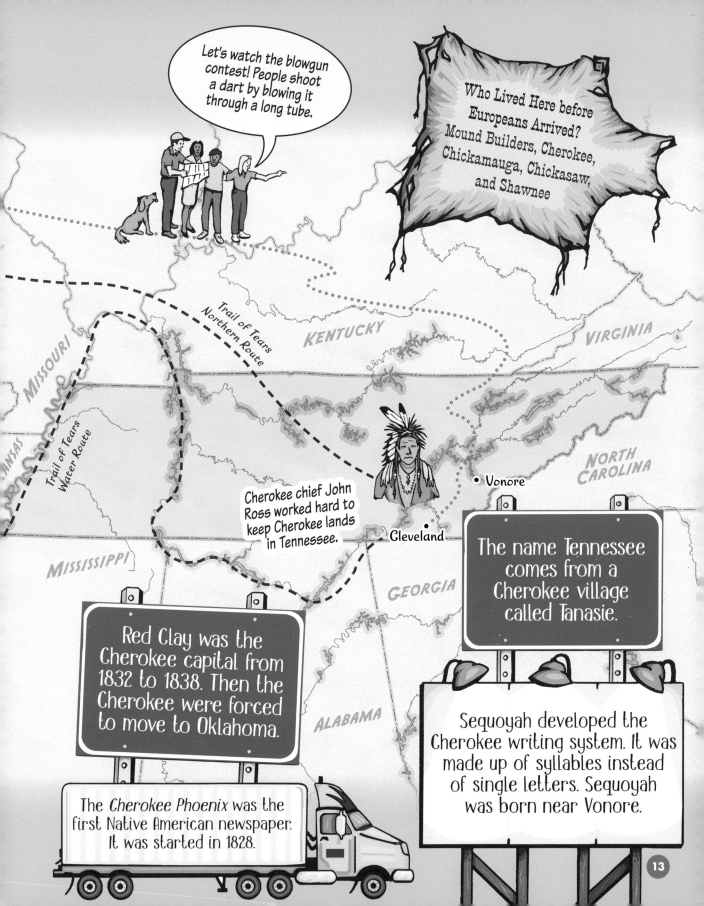

Let's watch the blowgun contest! People shoot a dart by blowing it through a long tube.

Who Lived Here before Europeans Arrived? Mound Builders, Cherokee, Chickamauga, Chickasaw, and Shawnee

Trail of Tears Northern Route

Trail of Tears Water Route

KENTUCKY

VIRGINIA

MISSOURI

NORTH CAROLINA

• Vonore

Cherokee chief John Ross worked hard to keep Cherokee lands in Tennessee.

Cleveland

The name Tennessee comes from a Cherokee village called Tanasie.

MISSISSIPPI

GEORGIA

Red Clay was the Cherokee capital from 1832 to 1838. Then the Cherokee were forced to move to Oklahoma.

ALABAMA

Sequoyah developed the Cherokee writing system. It was made up of syllables instead of single letters. Sequoyah was born near Vonore.

The *Cherokee Phoenix* was the first Native American newspaper. It was started in 1828.

People in eastern Tennessee formed the state of Franklin in 1784. It lasted until 1788.

Tennessee was the 16th state to enter the Union. It joined on June 1, 1796.

Look at those dolls! Kids made them from husks pulled off of corncobs.

MISSOURI

KENTUCKY

VIRGINIA

Kingsport

Piney Flats

Limestone

ARKANSAS

NORTH CAROLINA

GEORGIA

ALABAMA

MISSISSIPPI

Tennessee was once called the Territory of the United States South of the River Ohio. It was called the Southwest Territory for short.

Davy Crockett was a famous woodsman. He was born near Limestone.

Piney Flats was the capital of the Southwest Territory from 1790 to 1792.

PIONEER LIFE AT ROCKY MOUNT

Step into the log cabin. The oldest parts of the house were built in the late 1760s. Make your way to the kitchen. Try some food cooked over an open fire. Then visit the weaving cabin. You'll see how people spun and wove wool.

You're exploring Rocky Mount Museum. It's in Piney Flats. There you'll see how Tennessee **pioneers** lived.

Pioneers were really tough. They crossed the mountains into the wilderness. They chopped down trees to build homes.

Woodsman Daniel Boone cut a trail for pioneers. He began near present-day Kingsport in 1775. Then he continued on to Virginia and Kentucky. This was called the Wilderness Road.

Daniel Boone became a legendary hero of American history.

SHILOH AND THE CIVIL WAR

Visit with soldiers in their tent camps. Some wear blue uniforms, and some wear gray. They show how they fired their guns and cannons.

You're at Shiloh battlefield near Savannah. People are honoring the **anniversary** of this battle. It took place during the Civil War (1861–1865).

This war divided the nation. The North, or Union, opposed slavery. The South, or Confederacy, wanted to keep slavery. There were Tennesseans on both sides. But Tennessee ended up joining the Confederacy. Many battles were fought in Tennessee. When the Union won, Tennessee was the first state to rejoin the Union.

The Battle of Shiloh took place on April 6-7, 1862. The Union won a big victory there.

Reenactors dress as soldiers and people from the Battle of Shiloh.

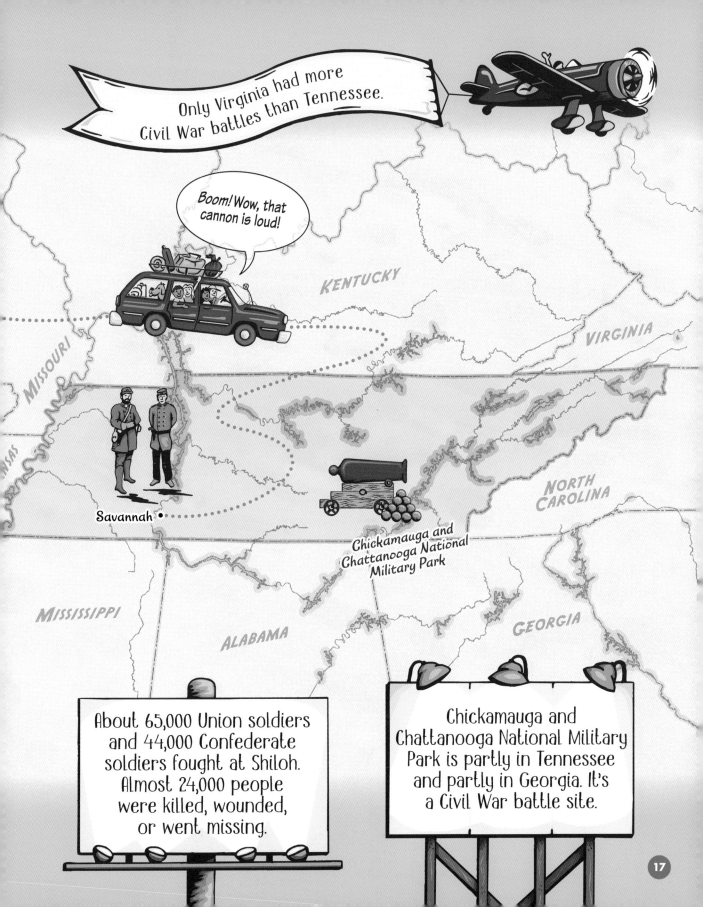

Only Virginia had more Civil War battles than Tennessee.

Boom! Wow, that cannon is loud!

KENTUCKY

MISSOURI

VIRGINIA

Savannah •

NORTH CAROLINA

Chickamauga and Chattanooga National Military Park

MISSISSIPPI

ALABAMA

GEORGIA

About 65,000 Union soldiers and 44,000 Confederate soldiers fought at Shiloh. Almost 24,000 people were killed, wounded, or went missing.

Chickamauga and Chattanooga National Military Park is partly in Tennessee and partly in Georgia. It's a Civil War battle site.

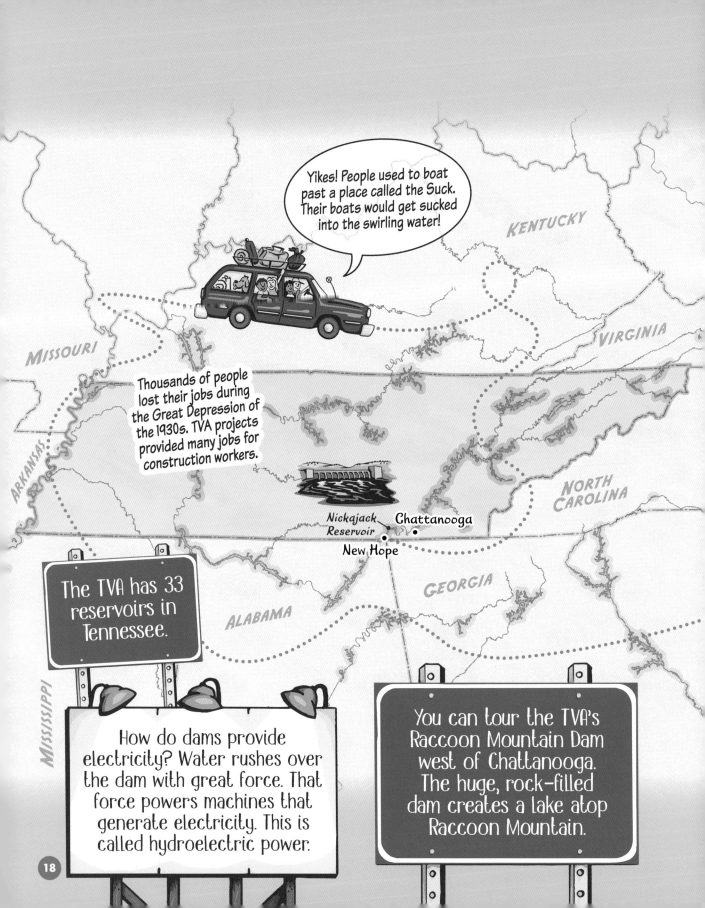

Yikes! People used to boat past a place called the Suck. Their boats would get sucked into the swirling water!

KENTUCKY

VIRGINIA

MISSOURI

Thousands of people lost their jobs during the Great Depression of the 1930s. TVA projects provided many jobs for construction workers.

ARKANSAS

NORTH CAROLINA

Nickajack Reservoir   Chattanooga
New Hope

GEORGIA

The TVA has 33 reservoirs in Tennessee.

ALABAMA

MISSISSIPPI

How do dams provide electricity? Water rushes over the dam with great force. That force powers machines that generate electricity. This is called hydroelectric power.

You can tour the TVA's Raccoon Mountain Dam west of Chattanooga. The huge, rock-filled dam creates a lake atop Raccoon Mountain.

18

NICKAJACK RESERVOIR AND THE TVA

Want to learn to paddle a canoe? How about a lazy float on an inner tube? You can do all this at Nickajack **Reservoir** in New Hope.

These waters weren't always so smooth. There were dangerous stretches with scary names. One was called the Boiling Pot! Boats could easily get wrecked there.

Nickajack Reservoir was created by damming a river. Tennessee has many other dams. The Tennessee Valley Authority (TVA) built most of them.

The TVA was established in 1933. TVA dams control floods and soil **erosion**. They make rough waters safe for boats. They also provide electric power over wide areas.

Tennessee's reservoirs make scenic canoeing spots.

Sit at the front of a bus. Listen to a speech by Dr. Martin Luther King Jr. Take your seat at the lunch counter. You'll learn about sit-ins. Some lunch counters served only white people. They refused to serve black people. Black students began protesting the segregation in 1960. They sat at lunch counters and would not leave when refused service. You're visiting the National **Civil Rights** Museum.

Many exhibits feature Dr. Martin Luther King Jr. Why? Because the museum building was once the Lorraine Motel. Dr. King, an important civil rights leader, was shot and killed there in 1968. The museum has a hopeful message, though. It shows that Dr. King's dreams live on.

He dreamed that all people could live as equals. He worked toward this goal all his life. His dreams still give people hope today.

A wreath hangs from the balcony of the Lorraine Motel at the spot where Dr. King was assassinated.

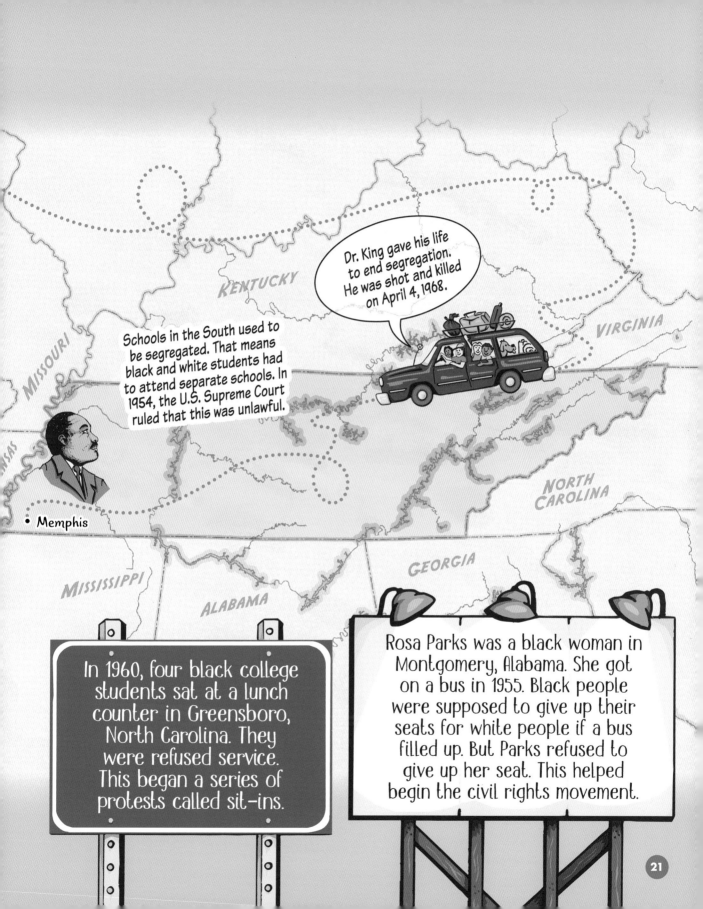

Dr. King gave his life to end segregation. He was shot and killed on April 4, 1968.

Schools in the South used to be segregated. That means black and white students had to attend separate schools. In 1954, the U.S. Supreme Court ruled that this was unlawful.

• Memphis

In 1960, four black college students sat at a lunch counter in Greensboro, North Carolina. They were refused service. This began a series of protests called sit-ins.

Rosa Parks was a black woman in Montgomery, Alabama. She got on a bus in 1955. Black people were supposed to give up their seats for white people if a bus filled up. But Parks refused to give up her seat. This helped begin the civil rights movement.

Tennessee has about 300 public libraries.

We can learn all about magnets. Look at all of the shapes and sizes they come in! Let's use a magnetometer to measure the strength of objects' magnetic fields.

KENTUCKY

MISSOURI

VIRGINIA

Oak Ridge

ARKANSAS

NORTH CAROLINA

The American Museum of Science and Energy explores peaceful ways to use atomic energy.

MISSISSIPPI

GEORGIA

The U.S. Department of Energy runs the Oak Ridge operations.

THE AMERICAN MUSEUM OF SCIENCE AND ENERGY

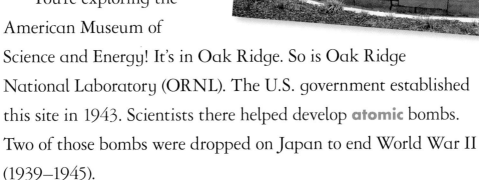

Meet some real robots. See how wind and water power work. Try some tests with light, sound, and electricity. Learn about science jobs you might have someday.

You're exploring the American Museum of Science and Energy! It's in Oak Ridge. So is Oak Ridge National Laboratory (ORNL). The U.S. government established this site in 1943. Scientists there helped develop **atomic** bombs. Two of those bombs were dropped on Japan to end World War II (1939–1945).

Scientists at ORNL are still at work. Some are finding ways to make the air cleaner. And others are finding better sources of energy. Would you like to work at ORNL someday?

Check out the Oak Ridge National Laboratory Visitor Center!

SPRING HILL'S MANUFACTURING PLANT

The Spring Hill Manufacturing Plant makes Cadillacs and GMCs. They use molds to create a car's body. They build engines. They paint cars. In 2017, the plant employed 3,679 people!

Motor vehicle parts are Tennessee's leading factory goods. Food and beverages come in second. Tennessee factories make cars, car parts, and boats. Chemical products are important, too. They include paint, medicines, and soap.

What's Mined in Tennessee? Crushed stone, coal, and zinc

Curious about how cars are made? Head to Spring Hill Manufacturing Plant!

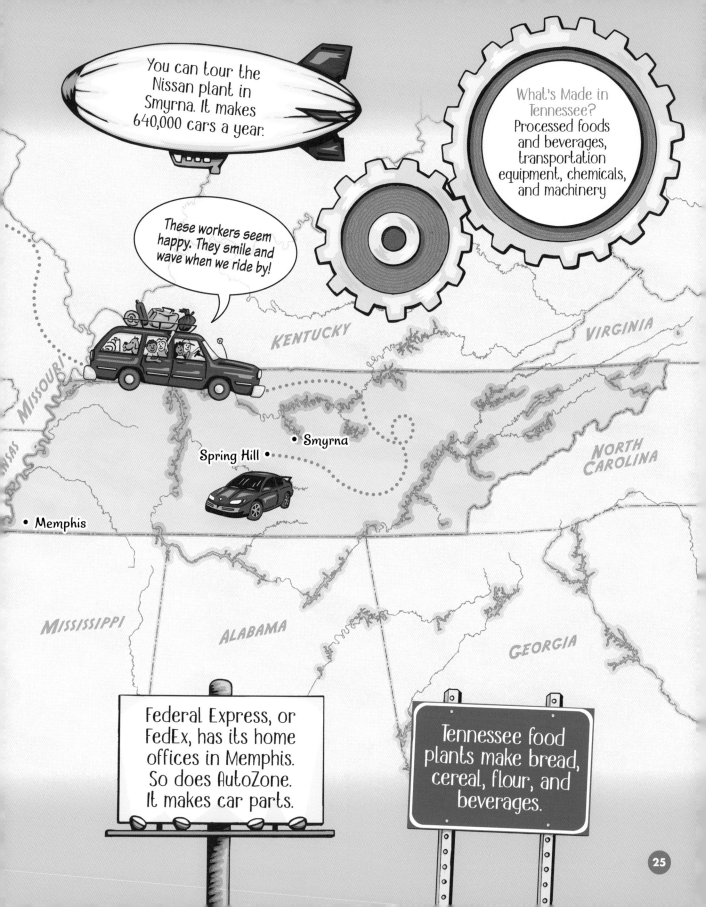

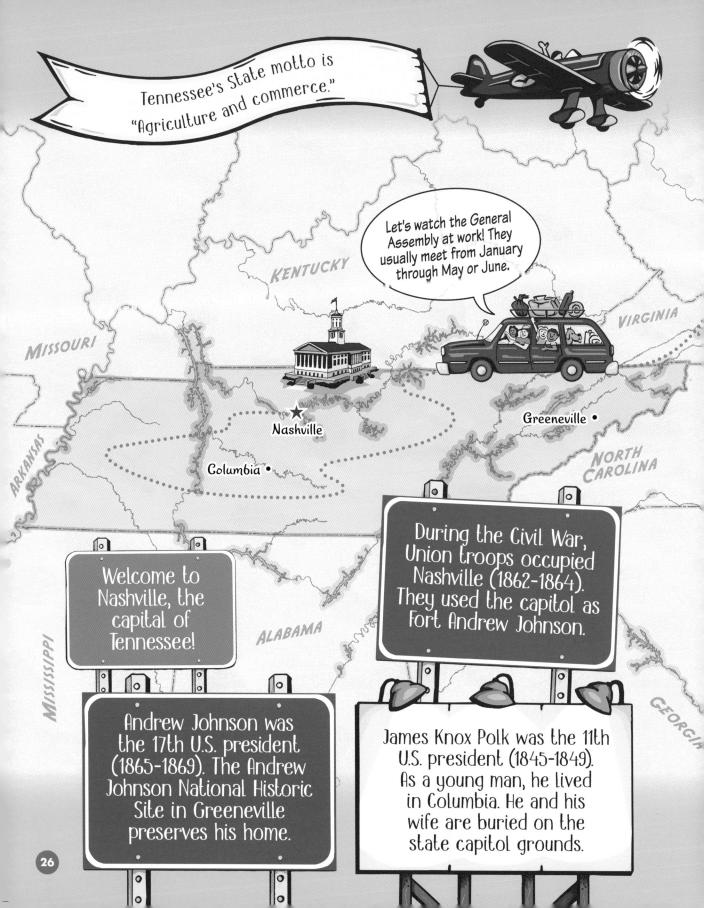

Tennessee's State motto is "Agriculture and commerce."

Let's watch the General Assembly at work! They usually meet from January through May or June.

KENTUCKY

MISSOURI

VIRGINIA

★ Nashville

Greeneville •

Columbia •

NORTH CAROLINA

ARKANSAS

Welcome to Nashville, the capital of Tennessee!

During the Civil War, Union troops occupied Nashville (1862-1864). They used the capitol as Fort Andrew Johnson.

ALABAMA

MISSISSIPPI

Andrew Johnson was the 17th U.S. president (1865-1869). The Andrew Johnson National Historic Site in Greeneville preserves his home.

James Knox Polk was the 11th U.S. president (1845-1849). As a young man, he lived in Columbia. He and his wife are buried on the state capitol grounds.

GEORGIA

I t's hard to miss the state capitol. It sits high on Capitol Hill. And a tall white tower rises on top. This grand building houses important state government offices.

Tennessee's government has three branches. One branch consists of the General Assembly. Its members make the state's laws. The governor heads another branch. This branch makes sure that people obey the law. Judges make up the third branch of government. They apply the law to court cases. Then they decide whether laws have been broken.

The capitol building was built between 1845 and 1859.

Many music styles found a home in Tennessee. Nashville is known for country music. The Grand Ole Opry House is there. Its country music concerts are broadcast on the radio. This is where many country music stars get their start.

More than 500,000 people visit Graceland every year. It was Elvis Presley's home in Memphis. Who was Elvis? The King of Rock and Roll!

Beale Street is another Memphis music spot. It's called the Home of the Blues. Blues musicians started playing there. By the 1920s, their music became popular. Stroll down Beale Street today. You'll still hear the blues!

Enjoy a night of music at the Grand Ole Opry House.

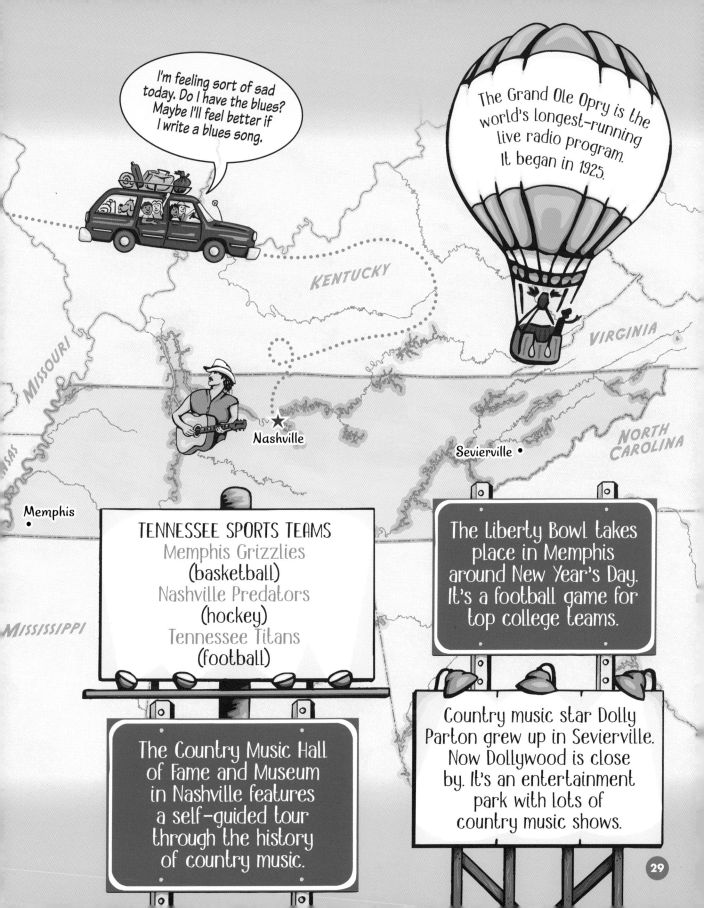

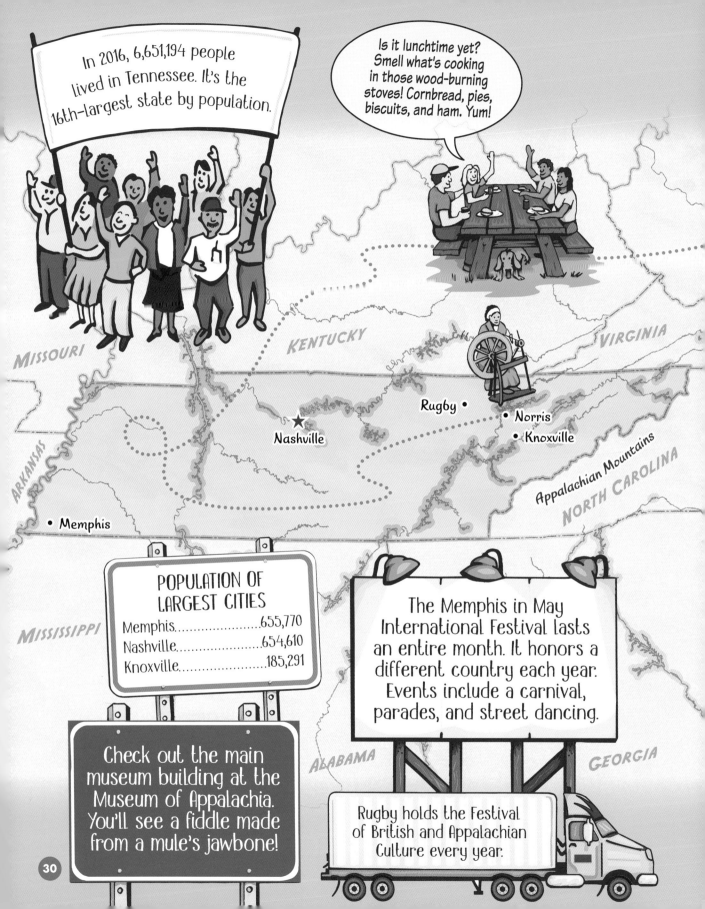

In 2016, 6,651,194 people lived in Tennessee. It's the 16th-largest state by population.

Is it lunchtime yet? Smell what's cooking in those wood-burning stoves! Cornbread, pies, biscuits, and ham. Yum!

MISSOURI

KENTUCKY

VIRGINIA

Rugby •

• Norris

• Knoxville

ARKANSAS

★
Nashville

Appalachian Mountains

NORTH CAROLINA

• Memphis

POPULATION OF LARGEST CITIES
Memphis......................655,770
Nashville.....................654,610
Knoxville.....................185,291

MISSISSIPPI

The Memphis in May International Festival lasts an entire month. It honors a different country each year. Events include a carnival, parades, and street dancing.

ALABAMA

GEORGIA

Check out the main museum building at the Museum of Appalachia. You'll see a fiddle made from a mule's jawbone!

Rugby holds the Festival of British and Appalachian Culture every year.

THE MUSEUM OF APPALACHIA IN NORRIS

Fiddlers and banjo pluckers play lively tunes. A horse or mule grinds sugarcane. People are churning butter and splitting logs. It's the Tennessee Fall Homecoming in Norris at the Museum of Appalachia!

Appalachia is the Appalachian Mountains. It includes the highlands of eastern Tennessee. Many pioneers settled here in the 1700s. They had come from England, Scotland, and Ireland. They brought their music and crafts with them. They developed an Appalachian culture all their own.

The Museum of Appalachia is a mountain village. There you'll learn about daily life in Appalachia. Wander from one log house to another. It's fun to imagine living there!

The Museum of Appalachia has many historic buildings and homes.

Where does ice cream come from? You'll get the scoop at Mayfield Dairy in Athens! It all starts with milk from a cow. Try milking a model cow yourself! Some milk goes into milk jugs. And some goes on to become ice cream. You'll see how the process works. Then you'll finish up with a scoop of your favorite ice cream at the ice cream parlor!

Milk cows are important farm animals in Tennessee. Beef cattle and chickens are valuable, too. Many farmers raise horses or hogs.

Soybeans are the state's top crop. Farmers also grow cotton, corn, and tobacco.

The Tennessee Strawberry Festival is in Dayton.

Some Tennessee cows make milk that will become ice cream.

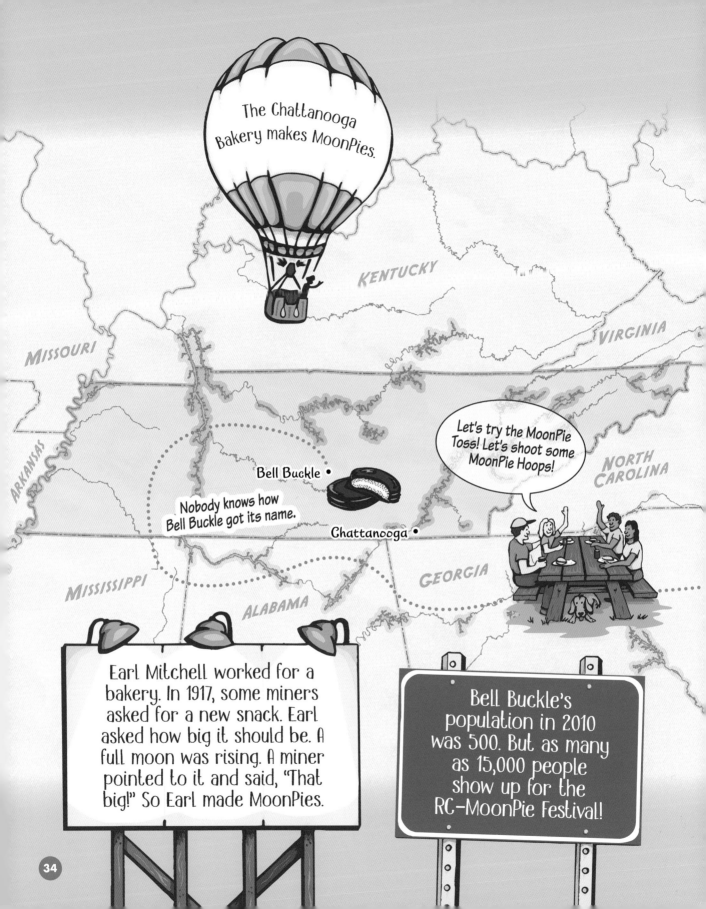

The Chattanooga Bakery makes MoonPies.

KENTUCKY

VIRGINIA

MISSOURI

ARKANSAS

NORTH CAROLINA

Bell Buckle •

Nobody knows how Bell Buckle got its name.

Let's try the MoonPie Toss! Let's shoot some MoonPie Hoops!

Chattanooga •

MISSISSIPPI

ALABAMA

GEORGIA

Earl Mitchell worked for a bakery. In 1917, some miners asked for a new snack. Earl asked how big it should be. A full moon was rising. A miner pointed to it and said, "That big!" So Earl made MoonPies.

Bell Buckle's population in 2010 was 500. But as many as 15,000 people show up for the RC-MoonPie Festival!

MOONPIE MADNESS!

Have you ever had a MoonPie? It's a yummy snack. It's made of two big chocolate-covered graham-cracker cookies. In between is a gooey marshmallow filling!

Does that sound delicious? Then come to Bell Buckle in June. You'll enjoy the RC-MoonPie Festival. It celebrates Royal Crown (RC) Cola and MoonPies!

Try out the MoonPie Games. Then get ready for the World's Largest MoonPie. It's carved up in pieces. Hungry people line up to get some. So get in line early. You might want to come back for seconds!

Try some MoonPies in Tennessee. Yum!

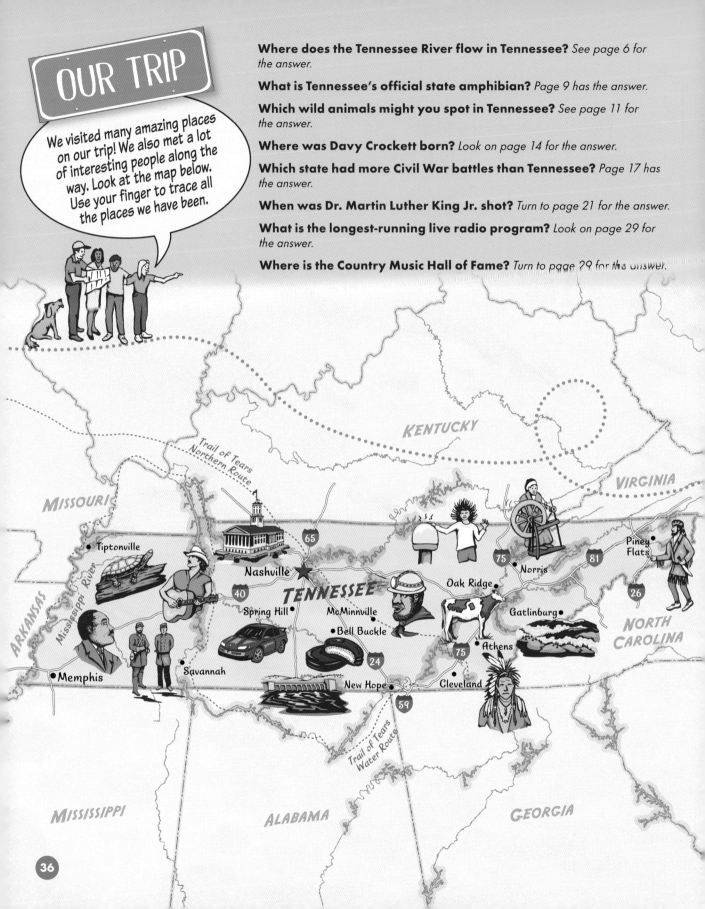

OUR TRIP

We visited many amazing places on our trip! We also met a lot of interesting people along the way. Look at the map below. Use your finger to trace all the places we have been.

Where does the Tennessee River flow in Tennessee? *See page 6 for the answer.*

What is Tennessee's official state amphibian? *Page 9 has the answer.*

Which wild animals might you spot in Tennessee? *See page 11 for the answer.*

Where was Davy Crockett born? *Look on page 14 for the answer.*

Which state had more Civil War battles than Tennessee? *Page 17 has the answer.*

When was Dr. Martin Luther King Jr. shot? *Turn to page 21 for the answer.*

What is the longest-running live radio program? *Look on page 29 for the answer.*

Where is the Country Music Hall of Fame? *Turn to page 29 for the answer.*

KENTUCKY

VIRGINIA

MISSOURI

Trail of Tears
Northern Route

Tiptonville

NORTH
CAROLINA

Piney
Flats

Nashville

Norris

Oak Ridge

Gatlinburg

ARKANSAS

Mississippi River

TENNESSEE

Spring Hill

McMinnville

Bell Buckle

Athens

Memphis

Savannah

New Hope

Cleveland

Trail of Tears
Water Route

MISSISSIPPI

ALABAMA

GEORGIA

STATE SYMBOLS

State agricultural insect: Honeybee
State amphibian: Tennessee cave salamander
State bird: Mockingbird
State butterfly: Zebra swallowtail
State flower: Iris
State folk dance: Square dance
State fruit: Tomato
State game bird: Bobwhite quail
State gem: Tennessee river pearl
State horse: Tennessee walking horse
State insects: Firefly and ladybeetle
State reptile: Eastern box turtle
State rocks: Limestone and agate
State sport fish: Smallmouth bass
State tree: Tulip poplar
State wild animal: Raccoon
State wildflower: Passion flower

STATE SONG

"MY HOMELAND, TENNESSEE"
Words by Nell Grayson Taylor, music by Roy Lamont Smith
Tennessee has ten official state songs. "My Homeland, Tennessee," adopted as a state song in 1925, is the oldest. The others are "When It's Iris Time in Tennessee," "My Tennessee," "Tennessee Waltz," "Rocky Top," "Tennessee," "The Pride of Tennessee," "A Tennessee Bicentennial Rap," "Smoky Mountain Rain," and "Tennessee (2012)"

O Tennessee, that gave us birth,
To thee our hearts bow down.
For thee our love and loyalty
Shall weave a fadeless crown.
Thy purple hills our cradle was;
Thy fields our mother breast
Beneath thy sunny bended skies,
Our childhood days were blessed.

'Twas long ago our fathers came,
A free and noble band,
Across the mountain's frowning heights
To seek a promised land.
And here before their raptured eyes;
In beauteous majesty:
Outspread the smiling valleys
Of the winding Tennessee.

Could we forget our heritage
Of heroes strong and brave?
Could we do aught but cherish it,
Unsullied to the grave?
Ah no! The State where Jackson sleeps,
Shall ever peerless be.
We glory in thy majesty;
Our homeland, Tennessee.

Chorus:
O Tennessee: Fair Tennessee:
Our love for thee can never die:
Dear homeland, Tennessee.

That was a great trip! We have traveled all over Tennessee! There are a few places we didn't have time for, though. Next time, we plan to visit Fort Nashborough in Nashville. It was built to protect and shelter early settlers. Visitors can tour the fort.

FAMOUS PEOPLE

Chesney, Kenny (1968–), singer

Crockett, Davy (1786–1836), frontiersman

Cyrus, Miley (1992–), pop singer

Franklin, Aretha (1942–), soul singer

Freeman, Morgan (1937–), actor

Giovanni, Nikki (1943–), poet

Gore, Albert, Jr. (1948–), politician

Handy, W. C. (1873–1958), blues musician and composer

Holt, Olivia (1997–), actor

Jackson, Andrew (1767–1845), Seventh U.S. president

Johnson, Andrew (1808–1875), 17th U.S. president

Parton, Dolly (1946–), country music singer and songwriter

Polk, James (1795–1849), 11th U.S. president

Presley, Elvis (1935–1977), rock and roll musician

Sequoyah (ca. 1775–1843), Cherokee scholar

Timberlake, Justin (1981–), pop singer

Turner, Tina (1939–), singer

WORDS TO KNOW

anniversary (an-uh-VER-suh-ree) a date that marks when an important event occurred in the past

atomic (uh-TOM-ik) using power released when tiny particles called atoms are split

caverns (KAV-urnz) caves

civil rights (SIV-uhl RITES) the rights that belong to every citizen

culture (KUHL-chur) a group of people's customs, beliefs, and way of life

erosion (ih-ROW-zhun) wearing away by water or wind

pioneers (py-uh-NEERZ) some of the first people to settle in an area

reservoir (REZ-ur-vwar) a holding area used to store water

robots (ROW-bohts) machines that do human tasks

State seal

State flag

TO LEARN MORE

IN THE LIBRARY

Adamson, Thomas K. *The Civil War*. Mankato, MN: The Child's World, 2015.

Glave, Tom. *Tennessee Titans*. Mankato, MN: The Child's World, 2016.

Rechner, Amy. *Tennessee: The Volunteer State*. Minneapolis, MN: Bellwether, 2014.

ON THE WEB

Visit our Web site for links about Tennessee:

childsworld.com/links

Note to Parents, Teachers, and Librarians: We routinely verify our Web links to make sure they are safe and active sites. So encourage your readers to check them out!

PLACES TO VISIT OR CONTACT

Tennessee Civil War National Heritage Area

tncivilwar.org
PO Box 80
Middle Tennessee State University
Murfreesboro, TN 37132
615/898-2947
For more information about the history of Tennessee

Tennessee Department of Tourist Development

tnvacation.com
312 Rosa L. Parks Avenue
Nashville, TN 37243
615/741-2159
For more information about traveling in Tennessee

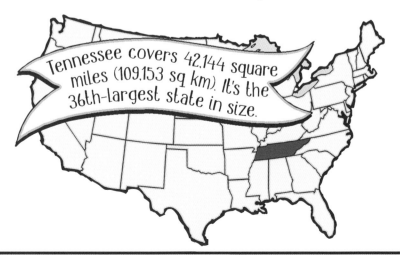

Tennessee covers 42,144 square miles (109,153 sq km). It's the 36th-largest state in size.

INDEX

Bye, Volunteer State. We had a great time. We'll come back soon!